W9-BNM-828

WALKING THE BIBLE

An Illustrated Journey for Kids Through the Greatest Stories Ever Told

by BRUCE FEILER

illustrated by SASHA MERET

HARPERCOLLINS*PUBLISHERS*

For Max and Hallie
Go forth

All biblical quotations are reprinted from *The Torah: The Five Books of Moses*, © 1962,
The Jewish Publication Society, with the permission of the publisher, The Jewish Publication Society.

Photograph on p. 25 © Adam Woolfitt/Corbis

Walking the Bible: An Illustrated Journey for Kids Through the Greatest Stories Ever Told
Copyright © 2004 by Bruce Feiler   Illustrations copyright © 2004 by Sasha Meret
All rights reserved. No part of this book may be used or reproduced in any manner whatsoever without
written permission except in the case of brief quotations embodied in critical articles and reviews.
Printed in the United States of America. For information address HarperCollins Children's Books,
a division of HarperCollins Publishers, 1350 Avenue of the Americas, New York, NY 10019.
www.harperchildrens.com

Library of Congress Cataloging-in-Publication Data
Feiler, Bruce S.
   Walking the Bible : an illustrated journey for kids through the greatest stories ever told / by Bruce Feiler ;
illustrated by Sasha Meret.— 1st ed.
      p.   cm.
   Includes index.
   Summary: The author describes his journey through places mentioned in the Old Testament.
   ISBN-10: 0-06-051117-6 (trade bdg.) — ISBN-13: 978-0-06-051117-3 (trade bdg.)
   ISBN-10: 0-06-051118-4 (lib. bdg.) — ISBN-13: 978-0-06-051118-0 (lib. bdg.)
   ISBN-10: 0-06-051119-2 (pbk.) — ISBN-13: 978-0-06-051119-7 (pbk.)
   1. Middle East—Description and travel—Juvenile literature. 2. Feiler, Bruce S.—Travel—Middle East—
Juvenile literature. 3. Bible. O.T. Pentateuch—Geography—Juvenile literature. [1. Middle East—Description
and travel. 2. Feiler, Bruce S.—Travel—Middle East. 3. Bible. O.T.—Geography.] I. Meret, Sasha, ill. II. Title.
DS49.7.F45 2004   2003015861
222'.1091—dc22   CIP
                                                                                                                 AC

Typography by Neil Swaab   ❖

CONTENTS

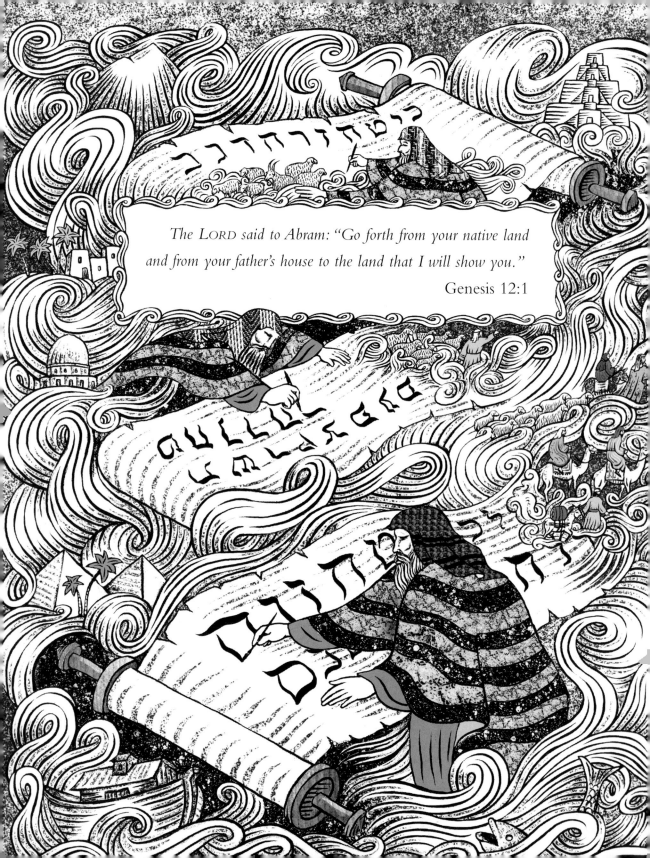

The LORD said to Abram: "Go forth from your native land and from your father's house to the land that I will show you."

Genesis 12:1

Walking the Bible

THE SUN SEEMS BIGGER IN THE DESERT. It sits in the middle of the sky, staring down at you wherever you go, like some single-eyed monster saying "I want you. I want you. You will not escape!" The idea of the sun as a friend does not exist here.

In this place, the sun is your enemy.

On a hot afternoon, I am standing on a hill, staring at the sun as it peers down on the most beautiful city in the world, Jerusalem. This ancient city—more than three thousand years old—is located in the central hills of Israel, in the heart of the Middle East, the region that gave birth to the Bible. The sun is white here, not yellow, and pushes down on the hills and valleys, which are mostly brown because there's so little water. A few palm trees climb from the stones. It's my first day in the city, and I am standing with my friend Fred, who wants to show me the many spires and domes that make up the skyline.

I grew up in the American South, in a city filled with churches and a wonderful old synagogue. I read the stories of the Bible, painted maps in Sunday school, and acted out biblical characters in plays. Yet somehow the stories always took place in some faraway land, in some faraway time that I could not entirely understand. The Bible was just a book to me.

After leaving home, I traveled around the world for years, living in Japan, England, and elsewhere. As I lived in these countries and tried to understand their cultures, the Bible became even less important to me. It was a book about the past. I was interested in the present.

Then I came to Jerusalem.

My friend positioned me in the middle of the hill. "Think back to your childhood," he said, "when you read the stories of our forefathers, Abraham, Isaac, and Jacob."

I did.

"Now look over there," he said, pointing to one hill. "That's a new neighborhood we're building today. Now look over *there*," he said, pointing in the other direction, toward the giant golden dome that marks the heart of the Old City, one of the oldest neighborhoods in the world. "That's the Dome of the Rock. And it's built on the rock where

Jerusalem

Abraham went to sacrifice his son Isaac."

For a second I couldn't speak. It had never occurred to me that the story of Abraham and Isaac—so timeless, so distant—might have happened in a place you could visit. It had never occurred to me that the story was so connected to the present. "You mean that story occurred in a *real place*," I said, "that you can touch—*today*?" In the Middle East, I realized, the Bible is not just a book. It's a living, breathing entity. The stories didn't just happen anywhere. They happened *here*.

Suddenly I wanted to know this Bible, the one that's connected to the ground. I had an idea: What if I walked across the Middle East, visiting the places where the stories occurred, and read the stories in those locations?

Could I even find those places? Did they still exist?

Over the next few weeks, I told everyone about my idea of retracing the stories of the Bible through the desert. Few people thought this was a good idea.

First, there were simply *too many* stories, people said, that took place over thousands of years.

Second, these places were unsafe, my friends back home said, because they were located in the Middle East—specifically Turkey, Israel, the Palestinian territories, and Egypt—places that are often filled with religious tension, terrorism, and war.

Finally, there was little archaeological and historical evidence linking these stories to specific locations.

And that was all before I told my mother.

But I couldn't get the idea out of my head, so a few months later I returned to Jerusalem. I went to see an old professor, an archaeologist who had been digging up biblical evidence for nearly ninety years. He was a short, gentle man, who sat hunched in a chair in an office overlooking the same golden dome that had been built on the spot where Abraham nearly sacrificed his son. He listened politely as I told him my idea, and when I finished he told me politely that I was out of my mind. "People like me are far too busy to talk to people like you," he said. I sat back, devastated.

But the professor was a generous man, too, and that night he called me. "What you need is a man with knowledge," he said, "but also a sense of poetry. What you need is Avner Goren."

The next day I went camping in the desert, where I met some young guides. I told them what I wanted to do. "What you need is Avner Goren," they said.

So when I returned to Jerusalem I telephoned Avner Goren, who agreed to meet me. Avner Goren is also an archaeologist, and he was in charge of ancient sites in the Sinai Desert, where Moses led the Israelites as they wandered through the wilderness for forty years. The next morning he arrived at the home where I was staying, driving a rickety blue Subaru that was older than Abraham. In his fifties, Avner had squinty blue eyes, a boyish grin, and curly gray hair that squiggled everywhere. His one distinguishing characteristic was a white scarf that made him look like a dashing adventurer.

We drove around the corner to a coffee shop. Avner was a charming, charismatic man, a child of the desert. I told him about my fears: Where would I go? Would it be safe? For every concern he had an answer. Finally I told him that everyone I met told me I was crazy.

"I don't think you're crazy," he said. "I think it sounds like fun."

I sat back, relieved. "Somehow I knew you would," I said. "And by the way, would you come along?"

Blessedly, he agreed.

I returned to the United States and spent the next year preparing for our journey. I read more than a hundred books about the Bible—its history, archaeology, geography, botany. I was amazed by how little I knew. Did Noah's ark land in Turkey or Iraq? Where was Mount Sinai? You mean manna grows on trees? The homework itself became part of the adventure. One bookshelf filled up, and I bought another. My friends worried about my new obsession.

Then Avner and I began planning our trip. Our biggest problem was that there is little archaeological evidence linking the stories to specific places. While scientists know a lot about how people lived during biblical times, they have no written evidence that says specifically that Noah lived in this place or that Abraham traveled over that road. Also, we faced the additional challenges of war, terrorism, sickness, and, of course, the weather. There are times of the year when it's so hot in the desert that one simply cannot travel there at all.

We settled on a guiding principle: our goal would be to take the biblical stories off the page and replant them into the ground. We wanted to understand the stories in their world. Rather than focus on *every* story, we would focus on stories we could understand better by being in the places themselves.

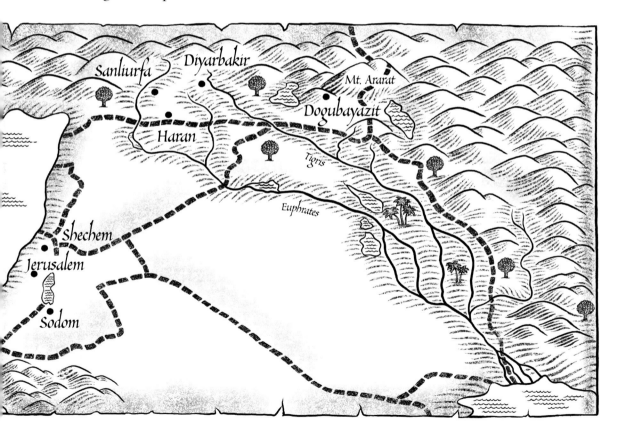

We would begin with the earliest stories of Creation, then proceed through the Garden of Eden and Noah, followed by the stories of the great patriarchs—Abraham, Isaac, and Jacob—before ending with the story of Moses leading the Israelites out of the desert and receiving the Ten Commandments. These stories are gathered in the first five books of the Bible—Genesis, Exodus, Leviticus, Numbers, and Deuteronomy—also

Avner Goren and Bruce Feiler

known as the Torah or the Five Books of Moses, because the Bible says Moses wrote them down.

After a year, Avner and I were finally ready to depart. We met again in Jerusalem and prepared to fly to Turkey for the start of our journey. I was scared. I had no idea what to expect. I had thought I was prepared. I had bought new adventure clothes, a new hat, and a new pair of boots. I had enough sunblock for forty years in the desert. But as I looked at Avner, who had simple bedouin trousers, messy hair, and sandals, I realized there was one crucial way in which I was not prepared at all.

All of my learning was in my head, I realized, and all of his learning was in his feet.

And the only way for me to gather his wisdom was to tuck my fears away and finally begin to walk.

When God began to create the heaven and the earth—the earth being unformed and void, with darkness over the surface of the deep and a wind from God sweeping over the water—God said, "Let there be light"; and there was light. God saw that the light was good, and God separated the light from the darkness. God called the light Day, and the darkness He called Night. And there was evening and there was morning, a first day.

God said, "Let there be an expanse in the midst of the water, that it may separate water from water."

Genesis 1:1–6

Creating the World

THE CALL TO PRAYER WOKE ME AT 5:15 A.M. It was a strange wailing sound that came through the curtains and jolted me from sleep. The words were in Arabic and were followed by smells—cinnamon, lamb, a whiff of burnt sugar. As I sat up in my bed in eastern Turkey, it felt odd to be starting a journey into the roots of the Bible in a place so different from my own. But as I dressed and hurried downstairs, I realized that my discomfort was similar to what many of the early figures in the Bible must have felt.

I was starting an unusual journey that I didn't quite understand, and yet somehow I felt called to go.

Outside, the sky above Turkey was murky and thick. A crack of lightning burst across the sky. Avner and I greeted each other and squeezed into the car we'd rented for our journey. Since the Bible begins with the story of Creation, we decided to begin where this story may have taken place.

The Creation verses tell the dramatic story of how God uses his power to create day and night, the earth and the seas, the animals and the plants, and, of course, human beings. One theme in the story of Creation is the importance of water. The opening sentence of the Bible says that when God began to create the heaven and the earth, a wind from God was "sweeping over the water." Later, when God creates the first humans— Adam and Eve—he places them in the Garden of Eden, which the Bible says is located at the junction of four rivers. There are no rivers in Jerusalem. Indeed, there's hardly any water at all.

So where do these stories take place?

One guess is that they take place in a rich, water-filled land to the north of Jerusalem, where two rivers come together to create a bounty of life. These two rivers are called the Tigris and Euphrates, and they are mentioned by name in the Bible. The area between the Tigris and Euphrates was called Mesopotamia, which means "the land between the rivers." The rivers today extend through Syria and Iraq. But they begin much farther to the north, in a remote mountainous area that very few people ever visit, in land that today belongs to Turkey.

That was the land we were traveling through now.

As we drove, the sky began to lighten, revealing a landscape of pistachio trees and cotton bushes. A turtle crossed the road.

Soon we arrived at the rocky banks of the Euphrates. The water was the color of mint ice cream and flowed rapidly. By the time we slipped our toes into the water, the sky was light but the sun was still hidden behind clouds. We had come for the sunrise, but we couldn't see the sun! Occasionally a ray would peak through, but then it disappeared. Finally, at a few minutes past seven, the sun prevailed. But it wasn't the color of sunrise. It wasn't orange or red or even yellow. It was clear, round, and white.

It was the sun of the desert.

It was hot.

We returned to the car and began driving east, toward the Tigris, which we hoped to reach by sunset. We were excited, but a little nervous. In recent decades

Euphrates River

this region has been one of the most dangerous in the world, with a local people, the Kurds, who want a homeland separate from Turkey. Even my guidebook warned, "In our opinion, travel is not recommended."

With almost no rainfall or major source of water, this part of Turkey is flat and dusty. Now, in late summer, the fields were dotted with green, and the crops sagged for lack of rain.

We began to discuss the importance of water in the ancient world. For most of human history, people roamed the earth in bands and foraged for food. This period was called the Stone Age. About ten thousand years ago, in what Avner called "the most important revolution in history," humans began to develop agriculture. That change occurred here first—in Mesopotamia.

Why was this agricultural revolution so important?

• Humans stopped wandering and settled in one place, planting crops for food.

• To make the farms work, they began to build canals to draw water from the rivers.

• With canals they needed laws and regulations.

• Since they no longer had to hunt for food all day, they had something new: free time.

• With free time, they began to tell themselves stories: stories about where they came from and where they were going.

The greatest and most long-lasting of these stories is the Bible.

—⧎—

By late afternoon we were close to Diyarbakir, one of the largest cities in Turkey's eastern region, located on the banks of the Tigris. Diyarbakir is also one of the oldest cities on earth, over five thousand years old. The Romans built a huge wall made of volcanic rock around the city when the city was already thousands of years old. The wall is one of only two man-made walls visible from space. The other is the Great Wall of China.

The town is grimy today, with a few beautiful Muslim mosques and a market selling carpets, spices, and tiny green bananas. When we arrived, the market was also filled with hundreds of plump watermelons. This week was a watermelon festival.

We quickly headed to the Tigris, which is narrower than the Euphrates, and muddier. A group of ten-year-old boys splashed in the water while an older boy watered some cows. A man tossed a net into the water and pulled out dozens of mullet, a small freshwater fish. We sat down on a boulder, and Avner pulled out a book. "Shall we?" he said.

I grabbed my Bible. I was nervous. This was my first chance to test the idea behind our trip. In addition to retracing the stories in the Bible, we planned to read the stories in the locations where they took place. We hoped this would help us to understand the stories better, but the truth is, we didn't know what to expect.

"Listen to the words closely," Avner said. "Listen for the sound of the rivers." He then began to read the first chapter of Genesis. He was reading the Bible in its original language, Hebrew.

Tigris River

"When God began to create the heaven and the earth—the earth being unformed and void, with darkness over the surface of the deep and a wind from God sweeping over the water—God said, 'Let there be light'; and there was light."

Avner was interested in one particular word in these verses that seemed a bit odd in English. That word was "deep." The word "deep" can best be understood to mean "deep water," he said. In ancient Mesopotamia, people told themselves stories about how the world was created, and as in the Bible, these stories begin with the idea that the world was covered in deep water. These stories say specifically that a sea monster lived in that deep water, who was then split into two pieces as the world was created.

The word for "deep" in Hebrew is *tehom*. The name of the sea monster is Tiamat. These two words come from the same root. Already the Bible seems to be saying that these stories didn't happen just anywhere: they happened here, in Mesopotamia.

We continued reading. For the next chapter and a half, the Bible tells the story of how God created the world. On the first day God creates light and dark. On the second day he creates land "in the midst of the water," and also the sky. On subsequent days he creates the earth and seas, the sun and stars, animals and humans. Finally, on the seventh day, having finished his work, God declares the day holy and rests.

The next story of the Bible shows an even deeper connection to Mesopotamia. In the second chapter of Genesis, God creates a garden for his first two humans, Adam and Eve. Then he sends a river to water the garden. That river is the Euphrates, where we had just been this morning. The story goes on to say that the Garden of Eden is located at the junction of four rivers. Two of those rivers are unknown, but of the two we can identify, one is the Euphrates and the other is the Tigris, where we were right now!

Though we were only on the first day of our journey, already I was putting my toes into rivers that appear in the earliest verses of the Bible. Already my dream was coming true.

The LORD God planted a garden in Eden, in the east, and placed there the man whom He had formed . . .

A river issues from Eden to water the garden, and it then divides and becomes four branches . . . The name of the third river is Tigris . . . And the fourth river is the Euphrates.

What's more, I already had a completely different understanding of the Bible than I'd had on the afternoon I stood on a hill overlooking Jerusalem. I understood the importance of water in the ancient world. I understood the power of geography in shaping the history of this region. And most of all, I understood the power of these stories. In a few short words, the Bible had taken the story of water, the story of humans, the story of Mesopotamia, and had created an entirely *new* story that explained the history of the world.

Stories, like rivers, give life.

Then the LORD said to Noah, "Go into the ark, with all your household, for you alone have I found righteous before Me in this generation. Of every clean animal you shall take seven pairs, males and their mates, and of every animal which is not clean, two, a male and its mate; of the birds of the sky also, seven pairs, male and female, to keep seed alive upon all the earth. For in seven days' time I will make it rain upon the earth, forty days and forty nights, and I will blot out from the earth all existence that I created. And Noah did just as the LORD commanded him.

Genesis 7:1–5

Noah's Ark

THE EARLY VERSES OF THE BIBLE are dramatic and colorful. God creates the world, fills it with animals and plants, and then adds humans. But almost immediately after he creates the world, God chooses to destroy it. He grows upset with how humans have treated his creation, and sends a flood to eliminate everything. "I will blot out from the earth all existence that I created," he says, including the animals and birds of the sky. But just before he does this, God chooses *one man* to save, his family, and one pair of each animal and bird.

That man is Noah. The way Noah saves the animals and his family is to build an ark that will withstand the flood. And the place where that ark lands is Mount Ararat. Because no place in the story of Creation has a name and the description of the Garden of Eden mentions only the names of the rivers, Mount Ararat is the first place in the Bible that can be located with any degree of certainty.

Avner and I headed there now.

The road east from Diyarbakir was creepy. Mud houses appeared, with stacks of tan-colored branches on the roofs. Turkeys scurried in the yards. Women with black veils balanced baskets of zucchini on their heads. We had a long way to drive before arriving at the mountain where Noah's ark landed.

We continued our conversation. With so much focus on rivers, it was only natural that floods would be important as well. The Bible tells the story of Noah early, in Genesis 6. After finding humans to be "wicked," God chooses to save Noah because he is "righteous," a good man surrounded by evil. He asks Noah to build an ark out of gopherwood (a hard wood from a kind of tree that no longer exists), divide it into three separate decks, and load it with one pair of every animal.

Then "all the fountains of the great deep burst apart, and the floodgates of the sky broke open." It rains for forty days and forty nights.

Scientists have been fascinated with this story for centuries and have asked many questions.

• *Where did all the water come from?* Some have said underwater volcanoes; others, melting glaciers.

• *How big was the ark?* The Bible says the ark was three hundred cubits long, fifty cubits wide, and thirty cubits high. A cubit is the length of a forearm from the elbow to the tip of the middle finger. That means the ark would have been the size of a soccer field, four stories high. (That would be five times longer than the *Mayflower* and half as long as the *Titanic*.)

• *Where did they put all the animals?* One student of the ark suggested that birds and rodents would have been on the top deck. Lions and tigers would have been on one end of the second deck, hippos and rhinos on the other, and elephants and giraffes in between. The bottom deck would have been empty, scientists at the San Diego Zoo concluded, because during their months on the ark the animals would have generated eight hundred tons of manure!

After seven months, Noah's ark comes to rest on a place the Bible describes only as the "mountains of Ararat." The exact country is not given. The ark then sits in this place for another three months before the water recedes enough so that the tops of the mountains become visible. Noah sends out a dove who eventually returns with an olive branch, a sure sign that enough dry land has appeared to support a tree.

For us, after two days of traveling across Turkey, the terrain became downright eerie. The mountains were covered in volcanic basalt and draped with green fungus. While cooling from a volcanic eruption, the basalt had splintered into hundreds of fists, which in turn had splintered into jagged fingers that reached to the sky. Together, the formations looked like frozen bodies grasping the air.

As we drove, Avner was busy punching numbers into a portable global positioning device. Finally he tapped my shoulder. "Look!" Just at that instant we rounded a corner, and far in the distance I could suddenly see the snow-capped summit of the tallest mountain in the region. It was about fifty miles away.

Mount Ararat

"That is Mount Ararat," Avner said.

Instantly I had a chilling sensation. Genesis does not give details about where the ark lands. It does not give the location on a map. But if a flood did cover the earth, if an ark survived that flood, and if that ark landed on a piece of earth, this would certainly have been the spot where it landed, because it's so clearly the tallest spot around. The Bible still lives in this place, I thought. I can touch it with my hands.

We drove down into the valley, to the town at the base of the mountain. Dogubayazit was the bleakest place we had been yet, with two asphalt roads intersecting in a neglected town of thirty thousand people. On the outskirts, hundreds of empty oil trucks were waiting to cross into Iran. Avner wanted to nap, so I headed alone toward the town center.

Hovering over the area, Mount Ararat is a perfect volcanic pyramid

16,804 feet high, with a junior volcano, Little Ararat, attached to its hip. The highest peak in the Middle East, Big Ararat is holy to everyone around it. The Turks call it the Mountain of Pain. The Kurds call it the Mountain of Fire.

In recent years, this region has been beset by war. The Turkish government actually closed the mountain to tourists because soldiers were smuggling weapons across it.

Though Dogubayazit was calm today, I was still nervous. I had barely entered the town when a man approached me eagerly.

"Hello," he said in English. We shook hands. "You just drove into town in that brown car, didn't you?" I was surprised he knew so much about me. "What are you doing here?"

"Um, I'm here to find out about Noah's ark," I said.

"Noah's ark!" he repeated. "Well, if you want to learn about the ark, you have to go to the green building at the end of this street. Go inside and up the stairs until you get to a dark room. Inside there's another set of stairs. Go up those and you'll find another dark room. In there you'll find the man who knows everything about Noah's ark."

At first I thought this was a trap and that he might want to harm me. Then I caught myself: Why exactly had I come here?

Inside the green building I found the sagging staircase and proceeded to the second floor. I found the dark room. I hesitated for a minute, then chickened out. I was just turning to go back downstairs when I heard steps from above. Seconds later a dark figure appeared. It was a man in his early forties, skinny, with black hair and an enormous bushy mustache. His eyes were concealed by the shadows. He examined me for a second before saying, in perfect English, "May I help you?"

"I was told you know about Noah's ark," I said.

"But you were supposed to go up the second set of stairs," he said.

I agreed.

"Maybe you don't really want to know."

He retreated as quietly as he had appeared and left me standing in the dark. This time I didn't hesitate, and followed him up the stairs.

Upstairs, the man settled into a low chair covered with carpets. He gestured for me to sit next to him and poured me a glass of tea. He wouldn't tell me his name but pointed toward his billowing mustache. "Everyone calls me Parachute."

We started talking, and after a while I asked if it was possible to climb the mountain.

"It is forbidden," he said. "Since 1991, nobody has been to the top."

"Is there anything to see?"

"If you believe something, you can see."

"What do you believe?"

"We believe. When we are children, they tell us that this is Noah's countryside. When something good happens, they say we have the luck of Noah."

"Do you have the luck of Noah?" I asked.

"I found something," he said.

"What is it that you found?" I asked

"Ah."

"You won't tell me?"

"Hmm."

As Parachute knew, stories of sightings of Noah's ark have been common for hundreds of years. In 1917, Czar Nicholas II of Russia sent two expeditions to photograph it. His daughter Anastasia is said to have worn a cross made of wood from the ark.

In recent decades, dozens of books have explored the subject. A former U.S. astronaut, James Irwin, led four expeditions to the top of the mountain, but never found his prize. I had asked Avner if he believed the ark would ever be found. He replied, "As a scientist, I doubt it. But as an adventurer, I hope so."

At the end of one hundred and fifty days the waters diminished, so that in the seventh month, on the seventeenth day of the month, the ark came to rest on the mountains of Ararat.

Which is exactly what Parachute hoped. With prodding he explained that during a trip up the north side of the mountain in 1990, he fell into a hole in the snow and found a piece of black wood one hundred feet long that he claimed was part of Noah's ark.

I told him I didn't really believe him.

"But the wood was five thousand years old," he said.

I told him I didn't really believe that.

"But we tested it."

We went back and forth for a few minutes when suddenly he let slip that he had pictures.

"Oooh," I said. "Would you show me the pictures?"

He wouldn't show me the pictures.

"But there are several billion people in the world who would like to know if Noah's ark exists!" I said.

He didn't react.

"Millions of tourists would come to this area . . ."

He didn't move.

"My mother is dying," I said (this was a lie), "and she could die in peace if she knew that Noah was real."

Nothing.

I was stunned. "Not even for my mother?" I said.

"You can tell your mother," he said, "that she can be happy. In the world there is one person who has seen Noah's ark. The Bible is true."

"So if she sees your ark, will she believe in God?"

"She'll have to," he said. "I have seen the proof."

Outside, darkness had fallen. I was upset by our conversation. I had no way of knowing whether Parachute had found Noah's ark, though I doubted it. But what was striking about what Parachute had said was that today, five thousand years after the story took place, little children who grow up at the base of Mount Ararat still talk about the luck of Noah. The spirit of Noah, like the spirit of the Bible, is still alive.

Abram went forth as the LORD had commanded him, and Lot went with him. Abram was seventy-five years old when he left Haran. Abram took his wife Sarai and his brother's son Lot, and all the wealth that they had amassed, and the persons that they had acquired in Haran; and they set out for the land of Canaan. When they arrived in the land of Canaan, Abram passed through the land as far as the site of Shechem.

Genesis 12:4–6

Abraham

THE BIBLE TELLS MANY STORIES—about the creation of the world, about geography, about nature. But above all it tells the story about the relationship between God and humans. Genesis is very careful to relate the history of the entire human family, from Adam and Eve through Noah to all the families of the earth.

Adam is the first human, of course. The Bible says ten generations pass between him and Noah. A generation usually lasts about thirty or forty years and includes an entire population of people of the same age. The next generation is their children, followed by their children. After Noah, ten more generations (three hundred to four hundred more years) pass before the arrival of Abraham, a man who serves as one of the most pivotal figures in the Bible—and one of the most important fathers of all time. Three great religions—Judaism, Christianity, and Islam—all consider this man the father of their faiths. Avner and I would spend weeks traveling through several countries, visiting the places where he walked.

We began in Mesopotamia, where Abraham was probably born.

After leaving Mount Ararat, we headed to the south of Turkey for the start of our search. Our first destination was Sanliurfa, a town not far from Turkey's border with Syria, where Abraham may have lived as a boy.

Abraham first appears in Genesis 11, and all we're told is that he's seventy-five years old, that he lives in "Ur of the Chaldeans," that he's married to Sarah and they can't have a child. Abraham is actually called Abram at the moment, and Sarah is called Sarai. God later asks them to change their names after they begin to worship him properly.

Avner said that the description of Abraham's birthplace, Ur of the Chaldeans, probably refers to the ancient city of Ur that was located near the union of the Tigris and the Euphrates. This would mean that Abraham was born near the Garden of Eden and that almost all of the early stories of the Bible take place in Mesopotamia. Scholars believe it likely that Abraham was born about two thousand years before Jesus—or four thousand years before today.

As is the case today, people in the ancient world did many things—some were farmers, some raised animals, others worked in shops. Abraham and his family belonged to a special group called pastoral nomads. Pastoral nomads did not live in one particular place, but moved every few years. They came to a place, set up their community outside the town center, raised animals, traded with the town, and then, after a few years, moved again.

The Bible echoes this way of life almost exactly. From the town of

Ur, Abraham and his family moved northwest through Mesopotamia over the years, up the banks of the Tigris and Euphrates rivers, until they arrived at the ancient city of Haran, which is located in Turkey today. In addition to animals—probably goats and sheep—they were traveling with a large family, including three generations—from grandparents to grandchildren. At this point, Abraham and his wife had no children.

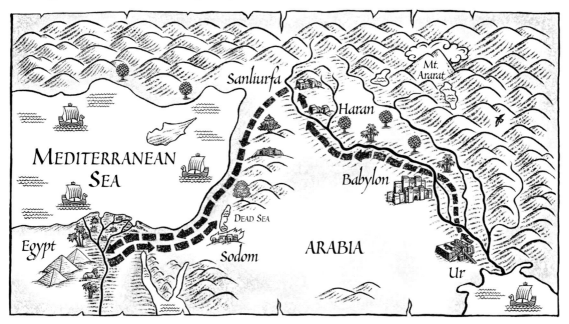

Sanliurfa, located just north of Haran, is a frontier town, with a large fort and an ancient castle. Local legends that have been passed down from generation to generation say that Abraham lived here when he was young.

When we arrived at the center of the town, we entered a small cave that had a lime-green carpet. Underneath a metal grate was a small pool. A guide explained that people come from all over the country to enter this cave, where they take off their shoes and collect holy water for their homes. To touch the water that Abraham may have touched can bring good luck to their families, he said.

The following day, our last in Turkey, we set out for Haran, the location of the pivotal scene in which God first speaks to Abraham. We drove south into the dustiest part of the country, on a road so straight it seemed to have purpose. Clay houses spotted the fields. Even army huts had roofs of mud. On the horizon a small bank of hills appeared, beyond which a valley extends down through Syria and Israel, and into Africa.

As we drove along, hypnotized by the landscape, I realized that this trip had begun to affect me in some place deep in my body. It wasn't in my head, or my heart. It wasn't even in my feet, though they felt pretty sore! I felt a deep connection to this land.

I mentioned this to Avner, who pointed out that the Bible says God made Adam out of dust. His name actually comes from the Hebrew word *adama*, which means "earth." Maybe I was connected to this place after all. Maybe it's home for all humans.

We arrived in Haran in midafternoon. We proceeded up the hill to one of the most barren places I've ever seen—a tiny village of about twenty huts buried beneath a coating of dirt the color of spoiled milk. On the outskirts of town were the broken pillars and overturned walls of an eight-hundred-year-old church that looked like one of those shipwrecks on the bottom of an aquarium. The centerpiece of the town was

Haran Ruins

some ruins that went back to the time of Abraham.

We climbed to the top of the ruins and pulled out our Bibles. After Abraham arrives in Haran, God suddenly speaks to him, saying, "Go forth from your native land and from your father's house to the land that I will show you." This is a remarkable request on God's part. He asks Abraham to leave *everything that he knows* but doesn't even tell Abraham where he's going!

So what does God promise in return? He promises that if Abraham goes on this journey, then he will give him what Abraham most wants: a child. What's more, he promises to make Abraham a "great nation" and to bless *all the families of the earth* through him. This is one of the most important moments in human history: God offers Abraham the chance to be his partner.

I will make of you a great nation,
And I will bless you;
I will make your name great,
And you shall be a blessing.

"This is the beginning of everything," Avner said. "The belief in one God. Abraham must leave everything behind and make a new start."

"So why did he do it?" I asked. It was late afternoon by now. The sun was starting to set, giving off the color of flames.

"Because God asked him to do it," Avner said. "He had no questions. He had faith."

"Do you think he was scared?"

"Weren't you scared when you started your journey?"

I nodded. I was scared thinking about the physical danger in some of the places we would visit; I was also unsure about whether our adventure would, in fact, bring me closer to the Bible.

"It's okay to be scared," Avner continued. "It's okay not to know. The story is telling us that. What's remarkable about what Abraham did is that he leaves the land of rivers, the land of water, Mesopotamia. In the Promised Land—down in Israel, where God tells Abraham to go—there are no rivers. There is little rain. But Abraham no longer needs the water. He has God. The message is clear: If we believe in God, we will be rewarded."

We sat silently for a few moments and watched the sun slide out of sight, leaving a layer of pink on the horizon. A herd of goats disappeared behind a hill. The dust had settled. For the first time since we started, I felt a sense of peace and calm. Abraham had walked here. He was scared and wanted a child. And yet he did the hardest thing imaginable: he left his father's family and went on a journey. He put his faith in God.

And he was rewarded with the largest family of all time.

And the LORD said to Abram, after Lot had parted from him, "Raise your eyes and look out from where you are, to the north and south, to the east and west, for I give all the land that you see to you and your offspring forever. I will make your offspring as the dust of the earth, so that if one can count the dust of the earth, then your offspring too can be counted. Up, walk about the land, through its length and its breadth, for I give it to you."

Genesis 13:14–17

Abraham in the Promised Land

THE ISRAELI SOLDIER stationed on Israel's border with Jordan eyed me squarely as we approached his post. One hand rested on his walkie-talkie. His other rested on his rifle. "Yes?" he said.

It was early one morning, soon after we left Turkey, when Avner and I strode toward the security checkpoint at the Damia Bridge, a few hours north of Jerusalem. We had driven up to the border that morning to begin the next phase of our journey, visiting sites in the Promised Land associated with Abraham, his son Isaac, and Isaac's son Jacob. The Promised Land bears that name because it's the land God *promised* Abraham in Genesis 12. Today that land covers several countries, including parts of Lebanon, Syria, Israel, Jordan, and the territories controlled by the Palestinian people.

Our destination this morning was Shechem, the first town where Abraham stops in the Promised Land. At the time of Abraham, the

Promised Land was called Canaan. The Bible does not say what route Abraham and his family took from Haran. It is most likely that he took one that passed through Syria, then crossed the Jordan River at the break in the mountains exactly where we were standing. We hoped the guards would let us walk across the bridge to see the view he might have seen. After hearing our request, the guard relayed our desire to his boss.

The border was bustling with life this morning. Trucks passed carrying oranges and honeydew melons. Guards would stamp their papers, then lift the gate. After a few minutes, a voice came over the walkie-talkie. The guard lifted it for us to hear. "I don't care if they write a book about the Bible," the voice said. "I don't care if they rewrite the Bible itself. But they're not going to do it in a war zone, and they're *not* going to do it on my bridge."

Disappointed, we returned to the highway and drove west, toward the mountains. The road began to climb almost immediately. The terrain quickly changed from bleak desert crumbs to garden-fresh greenery. Farmers stood by the side of the road selling tomatoes, cauliflowers, and radishes. Geographical changes like this are common in Israel, a country the size of South Carolina with a geography as diverse as that of the entire United States.

As with Turkey and all the other countries in the Middle East, the key to this diversity is water. The entire panorama of the Five Books of Moses takes place on the Fertile Crescent, a tiny strip of water-fed land in a sea of sand. I came to think of the Fertile Crescent as being like a person with his or her arms open wide, about to give you a hug. The upper arm of the Fertile Crescent was Mesopotamia, in today's Turkey, Syria, and Iraq. The lower arm was in Egypt, which is watered by the great river Nile. The middle of the Fertile Crescent—the Promised Land—includes today's Israel and Palestinian territories as well as parts of Syria and Lebanon. It is the heart and soul between the two arms.

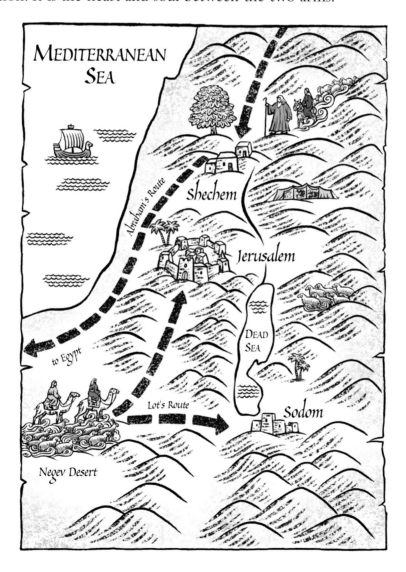

At the time of Abraham, Mesopotamia—with its abundant water—
was filled with strong countries with large armies. Egypt was the same.
The area in between was more fragile. There were no rivers, so there
were fewer farms and people. The two strong areas, Egypt and
Mesopotamia, fought with each other to control the middle. No one
ever did. Therefore, when Abraham came here, the Promised Land was a
weak place with a number of medium-sized cities.

Shechem was one of those cities.

The ancient city of Shechem is in ruins now, with a collection
of stones and ditches in an area about the size of a few city blocks.
Archaeology has shown that Shechem existed around the time
Abraham would have come here, but did not reach its peak until a few
hundred years later. The Bible says that when Abraham arrived, the city
was located alongside "a wise oak tree."

Avner mentioned that Abraham probably pitched his tent outside the
town. As a wanderer, he would not have been welcome inside.

"He must have felt very alone," I said. "He was far from home. He
didn't know what to expect. He was traveling with his wife, his nephew
Lot, and many animals."

"But remember, he had God," Avner said. "Genesis says that
Abraham did only one thing while he was here. He built an altar
to God. And God rewarded him, saying, 'I will give this land to your
children.'"

—⁓—

But there is trouble ahead. Abraham still doesn't have the child he wanted. He doesn't have a permanent home, either. And then famine stikes the land. There was little rain to begin with, which then stopped. Abraham and his family flee to Egypt. They stay there for many years and grow wealthier. Finally Abraham decides to go back to the land that God has promised them.

While in Egypt, Abraham's once tiny family has grown too big, with all its animals and newfound wealth. With such a large traveling party, Abraham decides that his nephew, Lot, has become a burden. So Abraham suggests that they split up, and he offers Lot the opportunity to go wherever he wants. Lot, of course, chooses the area of the Promised Land that has water, near the cities of Sodom and Gomorrah, leaving Abraham the drier areas near the desert. Abraham says good-bye to his nephew, but Lot would not be gone for long before Abraham stumbles into one of the most dramatic episodes of his life.

While Abraham is camped in the desert, three men come to visit him. Abraham is very gracious, fixes them food, and welcomes them into this tent. As they are leaving, the men reveal that they are messengers from God.

God then tells Abraham that he intends to destroy Sodom and Gomorrah

Lot's wife looked back, and she thereupon turned into a pillar of salt.

because they are filled with sin. But this is where Abraham's nephew lives! God agrees that Lot and his family can flee the hateful cities that he will raze to the ground, but he warns them *not to look back at the burn-ing city*. Lot's wife disobeys and looks back at Sodom and Gomorrah, and God turns her into a pillar of salt.

For years the site of this dramatic incident has been something of a great mystery around the Middle East. Where were Sodom and Gomorrah? People have hunted for years. Avner thought he knew, so on a warm afternoon we headed south out of Jerusalem toward the desert.

The Negev Desert, which occupies nearly a third of Israel's land, is dry, barren, and salty. About two million years ago, a massive earthquake caused a huge rupture in the area and left behind a giant scar across the face of the earth, from Lake Victoria in Africa all the way up to Syria. That's a distance of *two continents*! Part of that scar, which is called the Syrian-African Rift, forms the border between Israel and Jordan, and at the bottom of the rift is a large lake called the Dead Sea, the lowest spot on earth, 1,300 feet below sea level. As we approached, my ears began to pop because the elevation was so low.

The Dead Sea is one of the most unusual bodies of water anywhere.

• The air is hot and smells like sulphur.

• Because the Dead Sea is so low, the atmosphere blocks out dan-gerous sunrays, so the Dead Sea is the safest place in the world to get a suntan.

• Because of the air's heat, water evaporates at a faster rate, so the Dead Sea is 7 percent salt—six times saltier than the ocean!

• Because of the salt, it is said that you can float effortlessly in the Dead Sea. Don't believe it! When I tried, I sank so quickly that I almost swallowed the water.

But perhaps the most amazing thing about the Dead Sea was something I didn't discover until we began to walk into the desert hills on its southern shore. Because the atmosphere is so dense in the area, the air pushes down on the water and the water pushes down on several miles of salt deposits *underneath* the Dead Sea. These salt deposits are pushed down toward the core of the earth and then out toward the shore, where they sprout up in two- or three-story asparagus-like formations. They look like salt lighthouses.

Dead Sea

Salt Pillars

We approached one of these salt deposits, which felt scratchy against my hand. "Is it made *entirely* of salt?" I asked Avner.

"Lick it," he said.

I did, but pulled my tongue back in horror. It was indeed all salt.

This spot, Avner explained, is almost certainly the location of the lost cities of Sodom and Gomorrah, which may explain the origin of the story about Lot's wife turning into a pillar of salt.

Standing there, reading that story, I realized that the Bible is many things—a book of faith, a book of stories, a book of God. But it's also a guidebook, maybe the greatest guidebook ever written. The stories show deep knowledge not just of God and the characters, but also of the *actual places* where the stories occurred. Today we can take those stories to those places and feel much closer to the Bible ourselves.

Some time afterward, God put Abraham to the test. He said
to him, "Abraham," and he answered, "Here I am." And He
said, "Take your son, your favored one, Isaac, whom you love, and
go to the land of Moriah, and offer him there as a burnt offering
on one of the heights which I will point out to you."

Genesis 22:1–2

Abraham and Isaac

A FEW DAYS AFTER OUR VISIT to the Dead Sea, Avner and I woke up before sunrise and walked to the hill overlooking Jerusalem where I'd first had the idea to retrace the Bible. On that afternoon, my friend had pointed to the golden dome in the heart of the city and said that was the spot where Abraham went to sacrifice his son. Today we intended to retrace that famous walk.

The story of Abraham and his son occurs at a delicate time in the Bible. Though decades have passed since Abraham left Mesopotamia, he still has no son. Since Sarah can no longer have children, she decides to allow Abraham to have a son with her maid, Hagar. This practice was very common in the ancient world, Avner said. Hagar soon gives birth to Ishmael. Finally Abraham has a son.

But the story does not end there. Because Abraham and Sarah were so friendly to the messengers of God who warned them about Sodom and Gomorrah, God rewards Sarah with a child of her own. Though she is nearly ninety, Sarah gives birth to Isaac, whose name means "laughter." Abraham now has two sons.

This should have been a source of joy for Abraham. But it becomes a source of conflict.

Sarah becomes jealous of Ishmael and asks Abraham to kick him and his mother out into the desert. God promises he will continue to protect Ishmael, so Abraham agrees.

This is the beginning of the split that still divides the world today. Muslims consider themselves descendants of Ishmael. Jews and Christians believe they are descended from Isaac. But all three faiths agree that Abraham is their shared father.

At the moment, Abraham's problems appear to be largely resolved. He is living in the Promised Land with his remaining son, Isaac. But then God makes an unbelievable challenge. In one of the most controversial and heartbreaking scenes in the entire Bible, God asks Abraham to take Isaac, lead him to a hill in Moriah, and sacrifice him. In other words, Abraham is supposed to *kill* Isaac to show his love for God.

I had known about this story since I was a child, and, like many, felt very confused. Would God really allow Abraham to kill his child? Was it a serious request, or was God just testing Abraham's willingness to obey him?

Avner and I zipped up our knapsacks and set off down the slope toward the city. Jerusalem is one of the most amazing cities in the world—holy for half the people alive today. Jews consider the city holy because it was the capital of the country King David eventually set up in the Promised Land. Christians consider it holy because Jesus traveled and died here. Muslims consider it holy because Muhammad, their greatest prophet, traveled here as well.

Jerusalem has some of the best traits of other cities. It has hills, like Rome, and lots of beautiful old streets, like Paris. It also has some of the worst traits of other cities, including traffic like Bangkok's or Mexico City's. But it has light like no other place on earth. In the mornings and evenings Jerusalem is bathed in the most beautiful sunlight,

Jerusalem

which picks up the gold on the rooftops and the pink in the stones and charms anyone within its gaze. Seeing the sunset in Jerusalem reminded me of the feeling of warmth I had sitting by the living-room fire when I was a boy.

For Avner, who was born in Jerusalem and whose family has lived here for over one hundred years, Jerusalem is the most magical place on earth. When Avner was a child, his father used to take him on walks around the city and show him the sights of the Bible, just as Avner was now doing with me.

Our destination this morning was the oldest part of the city, which dates back to the time of the Bible. It's called the Old City and has narrow cobblestone streets. It is set on a hill and sur-rounded by a wall. The

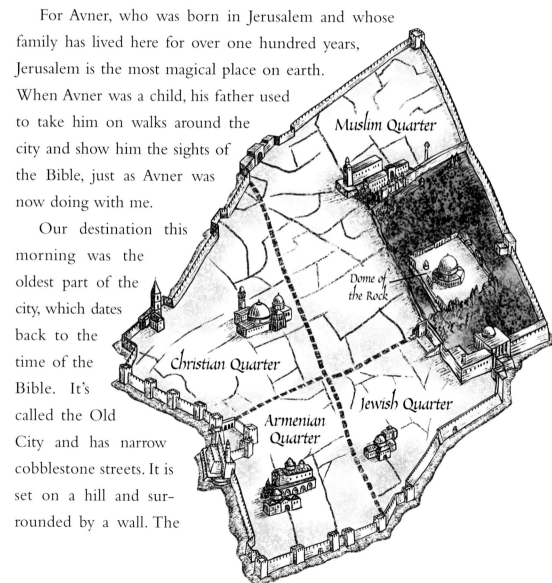

air is different up here, older and more mysterious.

It was late morning by the time we passed through one of the giant gates that lead into the Old City. We were approaching the holiest spot in Judaism, a spot that dates back two thousand years to the great Temple that once stood here. That building, constructed by the Israelites over a period of several hundred years, was the place where the descendants of Abraham ultimately stored the ark of the covenant that God gave them on Mount Sinai. The temple was destroyed by the Babylonians, rebuilt, and then destroyed by the Romans, and only a small portion remains. This is called the Western Wall, or sometimes the Wailing Wall because Jews who come here cry at the loss of their sacred building. Many people who visit tuck notes into cracks in the wall as a way of making a special prayer to God.

Next to the Western Wall is a ramp that leads to the highest peak in the city, the Temple Mount, one of the most sacred spots in the world. Jews, Christians, and Muslims all believe this spot is central to their religion. Legend says this spot is the first piece of land that emerged out of the water at the start of the world. And tradition also says that Abraham came here to sacrifice his son.

The park was calm this morning, with visitors wandering among the trees and kneeling in prayer. In the middle of the park is the golden Dome of the Rock, which Muslims built to honor the spot where their holy leader, Muhammad, departed for heaven. The dome is covered in 24-carat gold, and beneath it is the summit of the hill. It was on the spot

that the intended sacrifice of Isaac may have occurred.

We sat down and opened our Bibles. In Genesis 22, Abraham and Isaac arrive on the mountaintop. Abraham prepares a fire and ties his son to the altar. Then he raises his arms and prepares to kill his son. Will he? Will the great father of humanity, the man God chose to be his partner, actually destroy the son he waited his whole life to have?

At the last moment, an angel appears and tells Abraham, "Do not raise your hand against the boy, or do anything to him. For now I know that you fear God."

Abraham spots a ram in a nearby bush and sacrifices it instead. Isaac is spared.

This story has many possible meanings. Some people say God was only testing Abraham and would never have allowed Abraham to sacrifice his son. Others say the story shows that God's love for Abraham is just as strong as Abraham's love for Isaac.

As I sat on the Temple Mount, I realized that the story forces us to ask the same question that Abraham may have asked: Would I do what God asked of me, no matter how great?

When Abraham looked up, his eye fell upon a ram, caught in the thicket by its horns. So Abraham went and took the ram and offered it up as a burnt offering in place of his son.

Just the thought of this question surprised me. When I first started this journey, I was interested in questions of archaeology and history. Where did this story take place? What mountain was *the* mountain? Now I was becoming much closer to the people in the stories. It was as if I had entered the Bible myself.

Earlier, I probably would have doubted Abraham's resolve. I would have questioned whether he truly would have killed his son. Now I believed he might have done it. I doubted whether I would sacrifice *my* child. Still, I was surprised by how seriously I was prepared to consider the question.

And what about Avner, a father of two? I turned to him. "So would you have done it?"

He thought for a second. "Many times I have imagined how awful it would be to be a father in this situation. But I don't know. I don't know if Abraham would have done it, either. That's one of the mysteries of the story. But I don't think it matters. The point is to create the message of being devoted so deeply to God."

"And it works," I said. "This is one of the great stories in the Bible."

"It's like a crystal," Avner said. "You can look through it and see a hundred different angles, but none is more beautiful than the crystal itself."

Pharaoh said to Joseph, "Since God has made all this known to you, there is none so discerning and wise as you. You shall be in charge of my court, and by your command shall all my people be directed; only with respect to the throne shall I be superior to you."

Pharaoh further said to Joseph, "See, I put you in charge of all the land of Egypt." And removing his signet ring from his hand, Pharaoh put it on Joseph's hand; and he had him dressed in robes of fine linen, and put a gold chain about his neck.

Genesis 41:39–44

Joseph in Egypt

WHEN MANY PEOPLE THINK about the Bible today, they think about Israel. It is the heart of the land that God promised to Abraham. It is the site of many holy places. Jerusalem is mentioned in religious services dozens of times a day, all over the planet. People pray facing Jerusalem, they dream of Israel, they long to visit the Promised Land.

But the first five books of the Bible actually spend very little time in the Promised Land. The stories begin in Mesopotamia. They pass briefly through the Promised Land during the lives of Abraham, Isaac, and Jacob. But these stories all occur in Genesis, which is the *first book* of the Bible. The next four books spend virtually *no time* in Israel.

Instead, they move to the lower arm of the Fertile Crescent. Abraham, as well as his son Isaac and Isaac's son Jacob, all spend much of their time in the Promised Land. But beginning with Jacob's favorite son, Joseph, who is born in the Promised Land then sold into slavery by his brothers, the story shifts to the south.

To Egypt.

That was our next destination.

Traveling from Israel to Egypt is not easy. By foot it would take a month. By camel two weeks. By bus one full day. But for most of human history, this journey had been almost impossible to make because the desert that separates the two countries is so bleak. Many people have died traveling from one place to the other. In the movie *Lawrence of Arabia*, the main character makes this trip with two aides, one of whom dies when he falls into a pit of quicksand.

We decided to fly, which takes about thirty minutes. From the air, we looked down on miles and miles of desert. The sand looked like endless brown pillows lined up end to end. The ground was the color of chocolate. But then, suddenly, green appeared. Palm trees leaped from the ground like an army of artichokes. At first I was confused. Why all these trees in the desert? Then I realized: I was seeing the mother of all life in Africa. I was seeing the Nile—a river of mud between ribbons of green.

The Nile is to rivers what the Bible is to books: big, long, and important.

- The Nile flows 4,180 miles, making it twice as long as the Mississippi, the longest river in the United States.
- The Nile covers *one sixth* of the earth's circumference.
- The Nile floods every autumn, bringing valuable silt to Egypt's shores that creates some of the most fertile farmland in the world.

I had come to Egypt to explore the Nile's relationship with the Bible. Abraham's grandson Jacob had twelve sons. The eleventh, Joseph, was Jacob's favorite. Jacob loved Joseph so much that he gave him a coat of many colors, which made his brothers jealous. Why does Joseph get a coat and not us! they wondered. They decided to sell Joseph to slave traders, who took him into Egypt, where he landed in prison.

The story of Joseph might have ended there, but Joseph had a special skill. He could interpret dreams—he could take the mysterious images in a dream and explain what they meant in real life. The king of Egypt, the pharaoh, had a dream he couldn't understand involving seven fat cows and seven lean cows. Joseph was summoned to meet the

Thereupon Pharaoh sent for Joseph, and he was rushed from the dungeon. . . . And Pharaoh said to Joseph, "I have had a dream, but no one can interpret it. Now I have heard it said of you that for you to hear a dream is to tell its meaning."

pharaoh and explained that Egypt would have seven years of plentiful food, followed by seven years of too little food. The pharaoh was so impressed that he freed Joseph from prison and put him in charge of saving food from the fat years to use during the lean. Suddenly the great-grandson of wandering Abraham had become the number two leader in Egypt. How far the family had come!

Still, the story of Joseph raised a question: Where did the idea of dreams come from? We never heard about dreams in Mesopotamia. Could they be related to Egypt?

Our first stop in Egypt was Luxor, in the south. This part of Egypt is dotted with thousands of temples. Unlike Israel, where the monuments from this period in history are largely ruins, in Egypt the buildings are still standing. One reason so many survived is that they were covered for centuries with sands from the Libyan Desert, until archaeologists began unearthing them.

Walking around these temples today provides numerous clues to how Joseph may have lived. Indeed, many stories in the Bible are reflected on the walls of Egypt's monuments. For example, the hieroglyphics and carvings depicting the lives of the pharaohs show that Egypt brought many slaves into the country from outside the area. *This is exactly how Joseph ended up in Egypt.* The carvings also show that when political leaders were crowned they were given special rings and coats by the pharaoh. *This is exactly what Joseph was given when he became the second-in-command to the pharaoh.*

Perhaps the best example occurs underground, in the special tombs where the pharaohs were buried. The pharaohs were very wealthy, and they believed they would be able to continue to use their wealth, furniture, and jewelry after they died, so they were buried with their belongings. King Tutankhamen, often called King Tut today, was only nine years old when he became pharaoh—and only eighteen when he died. He was actually buried with dozens of artifacts made of gold, including some toys.

The tombs are long and narrow, like underground ant farms, and every inch of their walls is decorated with pictures of the pharaohs. Because the sun was so important to Egyptian culture, nighttime was particularly scary. The paintings show that the pharaohs hired special dream professionals to help them interpret what they saw in their sleep.

Aha! *Dreams were important to Egyptian culture, and now dreams are important to the Bible.* In the same way that the stories earlier in Genesis are connected to Mesopotamia, so the stories in this part of Genesis are connected to Egypt.

Before I left Egypt, I had to make one more trip to test exactly *how deep* the connection is between ancient Egypt and the Bible. I had to make one stop that I was very excited to make.

I had to visit the pyramids.

But why?

The pyramids are the most famous tombs in the world. They are the most famous Egyptian things in the world. They may even be the most famous *shapes* in the world. They are also famous because they are symbols of the power and grandeur of ancient Egypt. However, they are not famous because they're in the Bible. In fact, they're not mentioned in the Bible.

Or are they? For centuries, observers have suggested that the pyramids are hinted at in the early chapters of the second book of the Bible, Exodus. This book says the descendants of Joseph were building giant monuments for the pharaoh. Were these the pyramids?

Many of the pyramids are located a few miles west of Cairo, Egypt's capital, at the edge of the Libyan Desert. Pyramids, possibly from the Greek word *pyramis*, or wheat cake, are burial places for the pharaoh that are built in the shape of a sunray to allow the deceased king to climb closer to the sun god, Ra. In all, ninety-seven pyramids remain standing in Egypt today.

The three biggest are grouped together in Giza, and are the only surviving example of the Seven Wonders of the Ancient World. They would probably still make a list of the Seven Wonders of the Modern World. Try thinking of a list of the seven most famous man-made objects in the world—like the Statue of Liberty in New York City, the Great Wall of China, the Eiffel Tower in Paris, Big Ben in London—the Pyramids would be on anyone's list. Or, stop a hundred people anywhere on the planet and ask them where the pyramids are—it would be hard to imagine a score below 100.

The oldest and largest of the pyramids, built to house the pharaoh Khufu (or Cheops), stands 480 feet high and is known as the Great Pyramid.

- The Great Pyramid covers an area equivalent to seven square blocks in Manhattan, or twice the area of Times Square.
- The building uses 2,300,000 limestone blocks, each one about the size of a large refrigerator-freezer and weighing three tons.
- Lined end to end, these stones would pave a single-lane road stretching from San Francisco to New York.

The idea that the pyramids are connected to the Bible has been around for more than two thousand years. For much of this time, people were unable to read hieroglyphics and no one knew why the pyramids had been built. An English traveler in the fourteenth century wrote that the pyramids were used by Joseph to store grain when he worked for the pharaoh. Even as late as the 1970s, a prime minister

The Sphinx and Khafre Pyramid

of Israel said, "Our forefathers built these."

The idea comes from a passage in the book of Exodus. Genesis ends with Joseph reuniting with his eleven brothers and father and helping them to settle in Egypt. Exodus opens more than four hundred years later. The pharaoh who made Joseph a leader has long since died, and the new pharaoh is concerned that Joseph's descendants have become too powerful. He enslaves these people, who are called Israelites because they are descended from Joseph's father, Jacob, whose name was changed to Israel.

The Egyptians ruthlessly imposed upon the Israelites the various labors that they made them perform. Ruthlessly they made life bitter for them with harsh labor at mortar and bricks and with all sorts of tasks in the field.

These slaves are put to work building giant monuments to the pharaoh. Could the pyramids have been those monuments?

"Probably not," Avner said.

Abraham was most likely born around 1900 B.C.E. That means Joseph would have been sent to Egypt around 150 years later. Considering that 400 years then passed, the Israelites would have begun building pyramids for the pharaohs around 1400 or 1300 B.C.E.

But the first pyramid was begun around 2650 B.C.E.

That's 1,300 years *before* the Israelites came to Egypt. The Israelites did not build the pyramids.

So who *did*?

Many theories exist about how the pyramids were built, including speculations that the Egyptians used slaves, cranes, catapults, slingshots, crocodiles, or bulls. I have even seen books that say they were built by space aliens.

"Actually, it's not that complicated," Avner said. We know from ancient sources that the pharaoh used people, as many as 100,000, paid for by the government and organized into teams of ten. The stones were floated up the Nile on barges, then dragged to the site using rollers. When each layer was complete, the crews built a ramp of sand and brick to drag the blocks up to the next level. In the end, the pyramids are a good example of teamwork—and *hard* work—at its best.

But that raises another question: Why are the pyramids still so fascinating? The answer, I believe, is that no matter how many times you see them, they still make you happy. They have the endless ability to inspire. In that way, the pyramids are to Egypt what the Bible is to Israel: a timeless treasure that each generation embraces for itself.

Late that afternoon, Avner and I decided to descend the narrow passage to the heart of the second largest pyramid, built in honor of the pharaoh Khafre. We started down the shaft, which was no more than four and a half feet high. Claustrophobia quickly engulfed us. The deeper we got, the lower the roof became, until we were bending over like baboons, dragging our arms on the ground. I heard someone say that after making this trip he had "pyramid legs" and couldn't walk for a week. I could

Giza Pyramids

feel the air being sucked from the corridor and sweat dripping down my face.

Soon we reached the bottom of the corridor. We stepped into the chamber, about the size of a subway car, which once contained the mummy of the pharaoh. It was empty now, and very creepy.

"So let me ask you," I said to Avner. "If you could have witnessed one moment in the building of the pyramid, which would it be?"

"When they lowered the coffin into the tomb and all the stones came flooding in to fill the passageway."

"And if you could have asked one question?"

"For me, the question is not 'how?'," he said, "but 'why?' I know they built the pyramids so they could get closer to the sun, but still! So much time, and so much effort. Faith is a very powerful thing."

The same, I thought, can be applied to the Bible. We know people who wrote these stories down because they had faith in God. But still! So much time and so much effort went into creating the Bible. Perhaps it is no surprise that both the Bible and the pyramids are still powerful today.

Then Moses held out his arm over the sea and the LORD drove back the sea with a strong east wind all that night, and turned the sea into dry ground. The waters were split, and the Israelites went into the sea on dry ground, the waters forming a wall for them on their right and on their left. The Egyptians came in pursuit after them into the sea, all of Pharaoh's horses, chariots, and horsemen . . .

Then the LORD said to Moses, "Hold out your arm over the sea, that the waters may come back upon the Egyptians and upon their chariots and upon their horsemen." Moses held out his arm over the sea, and at daybreak the sea returned to its normal state, and the Egyptians fled at its approach. But the LORD hurled the Egyptians into the sea.

Exodus 15:21–23, 26–27

Moses Parts the Red Sea

WHEN I FIRST DECIDED to retrace the Bible through the desert, I had certain stories I was particularly eager to experience. First among these was crossing the Red Sea. The thrilling—unimaginable—scene in which Moses saves the Israelites from certain death by parting the waters of the Red Sea is one of the most magnificent stories in world literature. Jews read it at Passover; Christians at Easter. Even political figures like Martin Luther King, Jr., have quoted this story to support the idea that all people should be free.

But I faced some problems. First, no one knows precisely where the Red Sea was, though the general area is between Egypt and the Sinai Peninsula. Second, that area is unsafe today because Islamic terrorists live there. And third—well, how would I get across the water?

Still, I felt compelled to go, so early one morning Avner and I set off on one of our most hazardous expeditions. Because of the safety issue, we had to hire local guides, a driver, and a police escort. Five of us gathered in a jeep and set out east from Cairo.

Within minutes the scenery shifted from crumbling apartment blocks to mud-brick villages and farms. This is the Nile Delta, a triangular piece of land in which the Nile breaks into tiny streams. Imagine the Nile as a backyard rake: the river itself is the wooden pole, and the delta is the tines on the fork.

Because of all these streams, the delta is incredibly wet. It has always been Egypt's greenest region, where much of its food is grown. Today the vegetation seems to grow uncontrollably, in fields of cotton, rice, and corn. Water buffalo stomp through marshes filled with herons and storks. All this just miles from the Sahara, one of the most desolate deserts in the world.

This area, which the Bible calls Goshen, is the place where Joseph and his descendants settle. Soon those descendants have become so many that the pharaoh becomes concerned they will threaten him. He forces the Israelites to kill all their male babies. This is almost impossible to believe, but any Israelite mother who gives birth to a boy has to kill that boy so he won't grow up to father more children.

During this time, an Israelite mother gives birth to a son. To avoid having to kill him, she sets him in a basket and floats it down the Nile. The pharaoh's daughter finds the basket and adopts the boy as her own. She names him Moses.

Moses is raised in the pharaoh's home, but he learns that he has an

Israelite mother and father. One day he kills an Egyptian who has been tormenting an Israelite. Fearing for his life, Moses flees into the desert, where he hears the voice of God in a burning bush.

"Moses! Moses!" God says.

"Here I am," Moses replies.

"Do not come closer," God says. "Remove your sandals from your feet, for the place on which you stand is holy ground."

God then explains that he is the God of Moses' ancestors Abraham, Isaac, and Jacob, and that he wants Moses to return to Egypt and free the Israelites from slavery. Moses resists, saying he is not a great man. But God says, "I will be with you." Finally the reluctant savior agrees.

After Moses returns to Egypt, he asks the pharaoh to let the Israelites depart. The pharaoh declines. God realizes he must somehow persuade the pharaoh, so he initiates a series of "signs and wonders." These are called the Ten Plagues.

In the first plague, Aaron, Moses' brother, turns the Nile into blood. Then God overruns Egypt with frogs, followed by lice. Six more plagues follow: insects, pestilence, boils, hail, locusts, and darkness. All of this happens because the pharaoh refused to free the Israelites. Let them go and the destruction ends, Moses tells him, but the pharaoh refuses.

Scholars have long tried to figure out a scientific explanation for the plagues. One theory suggests that a comet passed too closely to earth, showering debris that was mistaken for hail and darkening the sky. An ecologist speculated that the plagues were caused by a flood triggered by heavy rainfall in Ethiopia. This would have filled the Nile with red clay, which is the color of blood. The red clay would have harmed the frogs, which would have died on the shore and attracted insects, and so on down the line.

Moses and Aaron went and said to Pharaoh, "Thus says the LORD, the God of Israel: Let My people go that they may celebrate a festival for Me in the wilderness."

These kinds of theories are interesting, but also frustrating. When I first started retracing the Bible, I, too, wanted to find a scientific explanation for everything. But now I realized that if we rely too much on science, we can forget the story. And the story is very clear on what what caused the plagues. God caused them. He wanted to free the people who worshiped him.

So God sends the tenth and final plague: he kills all the firstborn sons of Egypt, including the pharaoh's son. This persuades the pharaoh, who tells Moses to take his people and leave.

"Go, worship the Lord as you said."

The Israelites are finally free.

But as soon as Moses and the people depart, the pharaoh changes his mind.

By midafternoon, Avner and I had reached the end of the green area of the delta and found ourselves in open desert. The change was abrupt, and frightening. Suddenly the water was gone and we were surrounded by dry sand.

This is what the Israelites face when they flee slavery, only they are also being pursued from behind. Then they reach the shores of a new body of water, a large and mysterious sea. Water is in front of them; the Egyptian army is chasing them from behind. Only a miracle can save them.

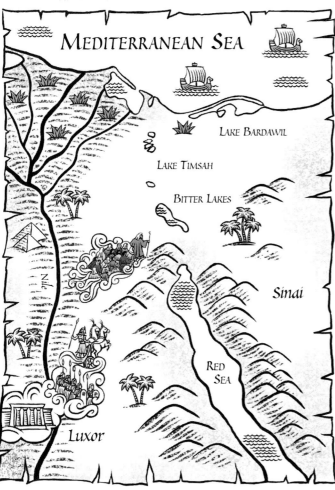

The Bible doesn't say *where* this sea was. There are five bodies of water that are candidates:

1. The Mediterranean Sea
2. Lake Bardawil, a marshy area just south of the Mediterranean
3. Lake Timsah, a large lake halfway between the Mediterranean and the Red Sea
4. The Bitter Lakes, just to the south of Lake Timsah
5. The Red Sea itself

The original language of the Bible is Hebrew, and the

Hebrew name for this body of water is *Yam Suf*. *Yam* is the Hebrew word for "sea," but *suf* is *not* the Hebrew word for "red." It's the Hebrew word for "reed," a type of water plant. In other words, the real name for the water is not the Red Sea, but the *Reed Sea*. Someone translating the Hebrew into Greek over two thousand years ago made a mistake that nearly every translation of the Bible ever since has repeated.

But this mistake actually helps us with our mystery. The reed that the Hebrew word describes is an Egyptian plant called papyrus, which grows only in fresh water, not salt water. Since the Mediterranean, Lake Bardawil, and the Red Sea are all salty, we can eliminate them. That leaves the other lakes. Many archaeologists think that the name Yam Suf probably refers to Lake Timsah, since it is shallower than the Bitter Lakes. One can imagine the Israelites wading across this lake while the Egyptian chariots get stuck in the mud.

We decided to try and cross Lake Timsah.

But we faced challenges. First, the great Suez Canal now cuts through this lake, meaning it can be filled with large ships carrying cars and oil. As we approached the shores of the lake, we noticed a number of these large tankers. Surely they would not help us get across the lake.

And then it got worse. It started to rain. We stopped by a park and tried to find a boat, but no one would help us. Perhaps I wouldn't make it across. Our Egyptian guides were unhappy and wanted to turn back. "Can't we keep going?" I pleaded.

Finally we rounded a corner and saw a small fishing village. "That's it!" I cried. We got out of the car, and I spotted a teenage boy in a row-boat. He agreed to row us across the "Red Sea." We piled into his boat, which was about the size of a bathtub—me, Avner, the local guides, the driver, the police escort, the boy, and his uncle.

All around us, the water was shallow, and you could see plants along the bottom. Huge sprouts of marsh grass blossomed from the banks. This was papyrus—the reeds of the Reed Sea! Suddenly I imagined Moses lifting his arms as the water parted. The Bible says the parting was so strong that God turned the sea into a "wall of water" on either side. Moses then led the Israelites across the Red Sea. As soon as they crossed, the wall of water collapsed and buried the Egyptians under the sea.

As we were crossing, I asked the boy, "So what kind of fish do you catch?"

"Mostly Moses fish," he said.

"*Moses* fish?" I repeated.

"I think it's a kind of flounder," Avner added.

Lake Tinisah

As we were speaking, the sun broke through the clouds. Suddenly the feeling of the scene changed. Normally, when we read the story of the Red Sea we feel excited that the Israelites are leaving slavery and going into freedom. But now I realized they may have had another feeling, too. They were leaving the most civilized place on earth—Egypt—for one of the most isolated—the desert. How frightening! But they trusted Moses. And most especially, they trusted God.

And suddenly I felt a deep connection to those people—to what they must have felt like when they were here. I felt a deep connection to this story—and to the dreams of all enslaved people who look to it for inspiration. And I felt a deep connection to this place. This was a place to feel afraid, I thought, and yet this was also a place to feel God.

"So what do you know about Moses?" I said to the boy.

"He was a prophet," the boy said.

"Yes, he's the one who split the sea," I said. "Do you think you can do that for us?"

The boy smiled and tugged a little harder. "Sorry," he said. "That's a miracle."

And for the first time since I began the trip, I started to cry.

Now Moses, tending the flock of his father-in-law Jethro, the priest of Midian, drove the flock into the wilderness, and came to Horeb, the mountain of God. An angel of the LORD appeared to him in a blazing fire out of a bush. He gazed, and there was a bush all aflame, yet the bush was not consumed. Moses said, "I must turn aside to look at this marvelous sight; why doesn't the bush burn up?"

Exodus 3:1–3

The Burning Bush

L IGHT. THE FIRST THING YOU NOTICE about the desert is the light. It's a white light, brighter than the beach in the middle of summer, that seems to wash out everything in sight.

The second thing you notice about the desert is the space. The scene is overwhelming, with the sand blowing against the ground, the bushes bent against the wind, and everywhere rocks, dunes, and mountains.

The last thing you notice about the desert is the noise. When I prepared for my trip to the Sinai to retrace the steps of the Israelites, I braced myself for silence. The desert would surely feel isolated. But once I stepped into the open sands, I was amazed by how much *noise* there was—the wind whipping through the mountains, the sand tinkling against your face, the rocks crunching beneath your feet.

The desert may be empty, but it's the least quiet place I've ever been. And the most exciting!

From the moment I crossed the Red Sea and set foot in the Sinai, I felt a sense of freedom. The Sinai is an unusual place, a giant triangle wedged between Africa and Asia. It's mostly empty, twenty-four thou-sand square miles of nothing but sand and rock—with only forty thousand people liv-ing in an area the size of Ireland (a country with a population of five million).

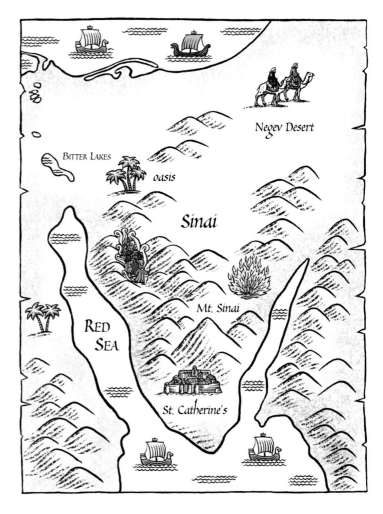

But I also felt a sense of unease. Being in the desert makes you unsure. You don't know where to sit, where to stand, what to eat, what to drink.

On our first night in the desert, we set up a campsite in a val-ley surrounded by hills that looked like molded clay. Avner said they were young by Sinai standards, only 400 million years old. During the day I had been so hot that I wore shorts and a T-shirt. Now I was so cold that I had to put on a pair of jeans, a sweatshirt, and a heavy coat. I quickly learned a lesson about the desert: the biggest problem is not the heat (you can escape that by sitting under a tent)—it's the cold. That's why even the bugs are dark, Avner said, so they can conserve heat and warm themselves at night.

We made a fire and ate flatbread cooked on the logs, tuna fish out of a can, cheese, and honey. As I lay down to sleep, I felt the appeal of the

Sinai Desert

landscape even more. The sky, which had been stark white during the day, finally emerged into a full bowl filled to the brim with stars. With no city lights, the stars were the brightest I had ever seen.

Once Moses and the Israelites arrive in the desert, they travel from oasis to oasis. We did the same thing. An oasis is a special area in the desert that has enough water to support trees and other vegetation. The desert has underground rivers that travel far beneath the surface of the earth. In certain places those rivers are pushed together by the mountains and squeezed upward. The water from those rivers is forced closer to the surface, making an oasis.

We stopped by a special oasis called the Oasis of the Tamarisk Trees. A tamarisk is a type of tree, with firlike leaves, that grows in various places in the desert. Up close, I could see that the wood was a reddish brown, like the coat of a fox. A camel was standing under one tree, eating the tiny green leaves.

We pulled out our Bibles. In their second month in the wilderness, the Israelites begin to complain that they don't have enough to eat. "Why don't you send us back to slavery!" they shout. God promises to rain down bread every morning and flesh every evening. The flesh turns out to be quail, and the bread a "fine and flaky substance" that the people call manna, from the Hebrew expression *man hu?*—"What is it?"

So what *is* manna? Some people say snow, others hail or dew. But there may be another explanation. In the spring, a certain bug (*Trabutina*

Tamarisk Tree

mannipara E.) crawls into the trunk of the tamarisk trees; eats the wood, which is salty; and spews out a white, sweet, sticky substance that forms into drops and falls to the ground. The substance is edible, but if you don't pick it up before midday it will melt. The residents of the Sinai call this substance *manna.*

When the fall of dew lifted, there, over the surface of the wilderness, lay a fine and flaky substance, as fine as frost on the ground. When the Israelites saw it, they said to one another, "What is it?"—for they did not know what it was.

The description of this substance is identical to the one in the Bible and suggests that there is a connection between the *manna* of the Sinai and the manna in the Bible. The feeling I got upon learning this was similar to the one I would have on first seeing Mount Sinai—the stories of the Bible are so connected to the ground, to the environment, and to the natural world around them that they seem more alive when you are in the region.

We continued toward the southern Sinai, the most dramatic place I've ever been. Here, red granite mountains soar from the toasty sands. The mountains are the color of sweet potatoes, and the light sparks off them in the late afternoon like the flash of a diamond.

And then, just when you think you've reached the end of the earth, a monastery appears. St. Catherine's Monastery was built fifteen hundred years ago by some holy men who believed that a particular bush at the

St. Catherine's Monastery

base of one mountain was the Burning Bush from which Moses heard the voice of God.

These men built a church, a library, and other buildings near this bush. The church is the oldest operating church *in the world*; they still hold services there five times a day in a language—Byzantine Greek— that no culture has used in a thousand years.

Avner and I spent a night here, each in a small wooden room with a single bed and a window. The eighteen monks who live here all go to bed early (their first service is at four thirty in the morning!), so it became quiet by eight P.M. I decided to take a walk. The air was chilly. I heard keys clinking against doors. A finch hopped quietly onto a branch.

I proceeded through the monastery until I came to a dark set of stairs. Suddenly I felt like a little boy: I was afraid to go down the stairs. I held my breath and managed to walk down. I knew that at the bottom

The Burning Bush

of the stairs there was a room filled with the skulls of all the monks who ever lived at the monastery.

I made it past the room, rounded a corner, and came face-to-face with a giant bush. This bush, which the monks claim is the Burning Bush, is a wild raspberry, like one you'd find in the woods. It was taller than I am, and spilled out of the wall like a raggedy mop. The monks say it's the actual bush that Moses saw, but the truth is that the bush used to be located across a small walkway. That's right: *they moved the Burning Bush.*

Still, I felt excited to be sitting on a bench next to such an important place. The sky was dark and the moon bright. I felt honored to be in a place with such a sense of history. For hundreds and hundreds of years, pilgrims of many faiths had come to this exact spot, stared at this bush, and imagined what Moses might have felt.

I was just closing my eyes and thinking how special I felt when suddenly off to one side, I noticed a fire extinguisher. At first I thought it was in the wrong place, but then I realized the unexpected humor: *was this in case the Burning Bush caught on fire?*

I tried to put the fire extinguisher out of my mind and go back to considering the beauty of the scene when suddenly a white cat with a brown patch over one eye jumped out of the Burning Bush and landed at my feet. The cat looked at me as if to say "What are *you* doing here?"—then screeched at the top of its lungs. I was so scared that I screeched back, then immediately ran back to my room.

The next day I climbed Mount Sinai.

On the third new moon after the Israelites had gone forth from the land of Egypt, on that very day, they entered the wilderness of Sinai. Having journeyed from Rephidim, they entered the wilderness of Sinai and encamped in the wilderness. Israel encamped there in front of the mountain, and Moses went up to God.

Exodus 19:1–3

Climbing Mount Sinai

T HE STORIES OF the Five Books of Moses are set in a wide variety of places: rivers, seas, deserts, plains, and, of course, mountains. Perhaps the most important place of all is Mount Sinai, where God delivers the Ten Commandments. The morning after seeing the Burning Bush, Avner and I woke up early and prepared to climb one mountain where many believe this occurred.

Mount Moses, as it's called, is like a tiger at dawn, a cat curled up in the shadows, its coat the color of pumpkin pie. At 7,455 feet, Mount Moses is not particularly tall (it's half as high as the tallest mountain in the Colorado Rockies), but it is impressive, rising straight from the ground and softening slightly at the top, like a wet sand castle.

We decided to ride camels halfway up the mountain, then climb the rest of the way to the summit.

Camels are important to life in the desert because they are the only mammals capable of surviving without water for up to two weeks in the summer and two months in the winter. Camels don't store water in their humps—in fact, they don't store water at all. Humans need water to cool themselves down and maintain a steady body temperature. Camels don't need water because they constantly adjust their body temperature to match the climate.

Camels have other features that make them suited to life in the desert. In their humps they store fat, which they use as food. They have broad feet that allow them to walk in the sand without sinking. And they have two sets of eyelids to keep out sand. They also have the longest eyelashes of any animal alive. I have long eyelashes, too, so when I swung atop my camel I hoped my animal would think we were somehow related and not toss me off.

The story of Moses encountering God on Mount Sinai is one of the most beloved in the Bible. In the third month after crossing the Red Sea, Moses leads the Israelites to the base of Mount Sinai, which is covered in clouds and shakes violently. God calls Moses to the top of the mountain, where he reveals the Ten Commandments. Different religions list the commandments in

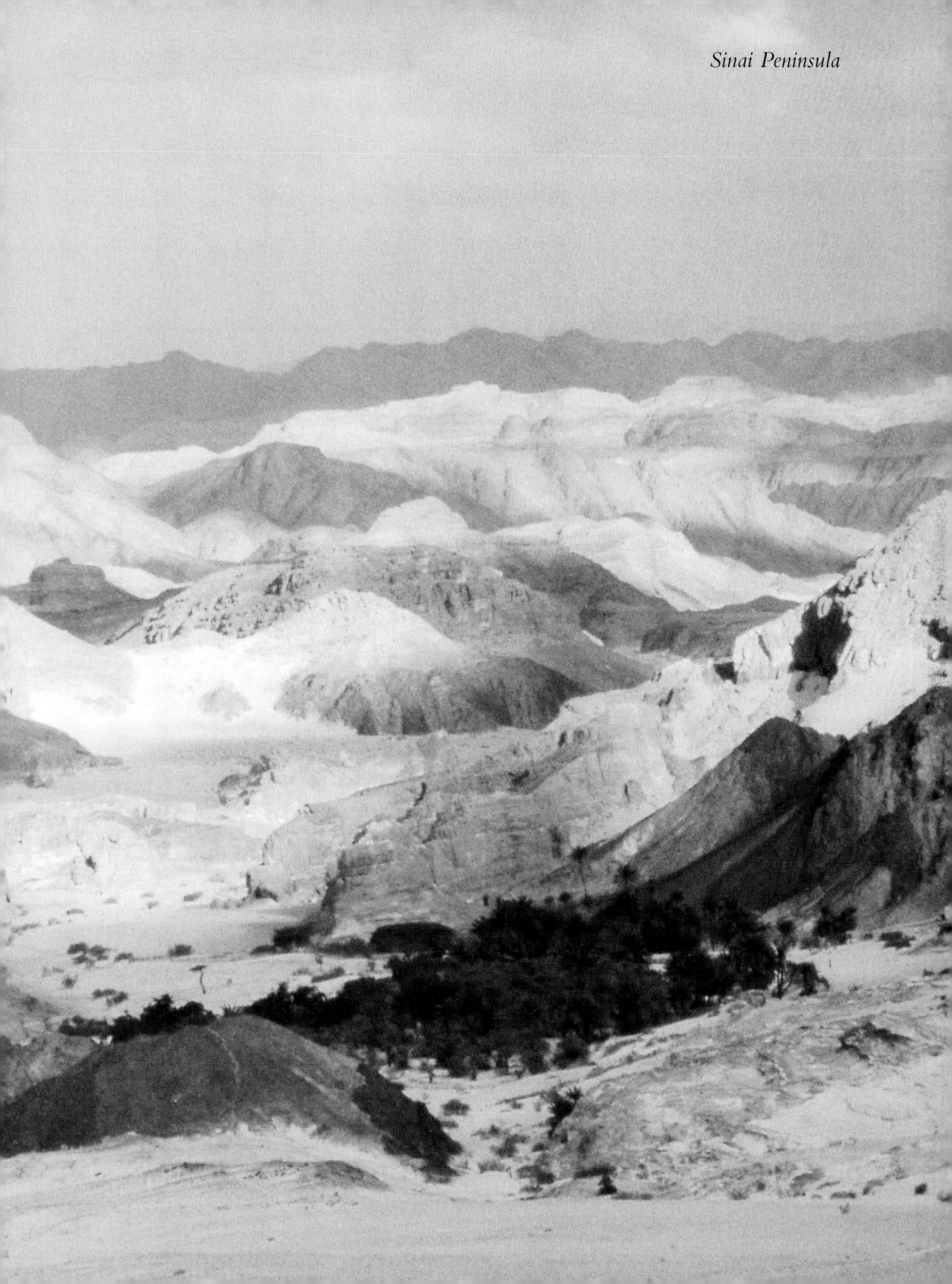

Sinai Peninsula

slightly different ways, but they convey the same basic information:

1. There is only one God.

2. You should not make idols.

3. You should not take God's name in vain.

4. Remember the Sabbath.

5. You should honor your mother and father.

6. Don't murder.

7. Don't commit adultery.

8. Don't steal.

9. Don't mistreat your neighbor.

10. Don't covet your neighbor's belongings.

This event marks the climax of the Five Books of Moses. Until now, the Israelites have received gifts from God—the splitting of the Red Sea, manna from heaven. Now they become participants in a legal relationship with God. They become the people of God.

But where did this great event occur? The Bible is silent on the matter, saying only that it occurs on a mountain in "the desert of Sinai." One legend says the mountains of the world quarreled with each other to host God. Each one said how great it was except for Sinai, which humbly said, "I am low." God chose Sinai, since it was the most modest.

Scientists have offered twenty-two different candidates for the real Mount Sinai, located everywhere from Egypt to the Sinai, from Israel to Saudi Arabia. So many choices! How could you ever know where it really was? At this point in my journey, though, I was beginning to consider a different possibility. Maybe the Bible doesn't want us to know. Maybe it keeps the location unclear on purpose. Maybe it wants this important event to occur in an unknown place, in a place open to all, in a space that is holy to everyone.

Maybe it wants Mount Sinai to be a place that we always dream of, but never find.

Climbing this particular mountain has meaning because for fifteen hundred years, pilgrims have come here *believing* it to be Mount Sinai. By midday Avner and I had reached the middle of the mountain, and we paused to have lunch in front of an old well. During the Middle Ages, this mountain was so holy that hundreds of monks actually lived on it to be closer to God.

Finally we were ready to resume our climb to the peak. The summit of Mount Moses is actually the crater of an extinct volcano that is darker than the rest of the mountain.

The path began to crumble fairly quickly, and within minutes I was crawling on my hands and knees, like a squirrel on a tree. I would grab a boulder with my left hand, wait to see if it would hold, then push myself upwards with a quick prayer. It was like climbing an avalanche of oversized popcorn.

"I can't believe Moses made this walk in sandals," I said.

After a while I was sweating through my windbreaker and almost completely out of breath. I pulled myself up one last boulder and came to rest on a flat area. The blush of the sun was gentle at this hour, and the air contained a hint of cold.

The summit was crowded, with a church, a mosque, and several tents where locals sold snacks to climbers. I half expected to see a sign that said MOSES SLEPT HERE.

The buildings are overshadowed by the view, a gorgeous panorama of blood-colored mountains and the Red Sea far away. The jagged mountains looked like the head of a giant lion roaring in the middle of the desert, each of the peaks another tooth tearing at the sky. A French artist once put it this way: "If I had to represent the end of the world, I would model it from Mount Sinai."

Avner went off to greet a bedouin vendor he knew, and I sat down and tried to recall what had brought me here.

When I first came up with the idea of retracing the Bible, I didn't know what to expect. I wanted to understand the Bible. But now I realized that I had learned so much more.

First, I had learned that the Bible is deeply connected to geography. When I think of the Bible now, I don't think of a book. I think of a map. I think of the family at the heart of the story, beginning in Mesopotamia, traveling down to the Promised Land, continuing down to Egypt, then passing forty years in the desert before returning to the Promised Land. This journey has a beautiful balance that I never understood before visiting these places.

Top of Mount Sinai

Second, I thought of all the countries I'd been to. There were empires and religions in Mesopotamia; they are gone. There was an empire and a religion in Egypt; they are gone. Yet the Bible—and the religions that grew out of it—survive. Why? Because the Israelites took the best of Mesopotamian culture, took the best of Egyptian culture, and introduced the idea that there is only *one* God. That's why biblical religion survives.

Finally, and perhaps most important, I felt a deep connection to those places. I felt stronger because of my journey, as if I had grown a third leg. I could stand more firmly on the ground. The best way to describe that feeling is to say that these places—the rivers of Mesopotamia, Mount Ararat, Jerusalem, the Red Sea, Mount Sinai—live inside my body, just as the stories of the Bible live inside my body. They are a part of me, and I am a part of them.

This was the great discovery of my experience. We don't have to walk the Bible to get close to the Bible. We carry the Bible around within us.

By late afternoon a haze had settled over the mountains. The sun was still yellow despite the dust. As I looked out over the plain, I thought again about the story of the Ten Commandments. Moses is on the mountain so long that his people believe he will never come down again. They build a golden calf—an idol—and begin to worship it instead.

God is so upset that he wants to kill all the people. Moses is so upset that he throws the tablets on which Ten Commandments are inscribed onto the ground. This is a crucial moment: Will the people, God, and Moses start fighting with one another?

The answer is no.

Moses realizes he needs the Israelites as his family. God realizes the Israelites are his people. And the people realize that God still loves them and will be their

When He finished speaking with him on Mount Sinai, He gave Moses the two tablets of the Pact, stone tablets inscribed with the finger of God.

protector. Once this partnership is formed, the remainder of human history is set. No matter what would happen in the future, God and humans were united forever, and that bond was sealed on Mount Sinai.

Staring out at the sun just dipping below the horizon, I realized that *my* journey was sealed here as well. I, too, was part of the same bond. No matter what would happen in my future, I had become part of the story. I, too, would set out from here, secure in my relationship with the roots of the Bible and prepared for the promise to come.

And the People Believed

Fred Benjamin gave the tour that inspired this project. Laura Benjamin was a loyal and generous friend. Yael and Noah Benjamin were in my mind as I wrote this book, just as I camped in their bedroom often as I lived it.

This story is a tribute to the wisdom, experience, and good humor of Avner Goren. Jane Friedman encouraged this idea with enthusiasm. David Black, Trish Grader, Stephen Hildreth, and especially the talented Alix Reid helped bring it to living color. Linda Rottenberg inspired me during the travels for this project, and just before its completion, became my wife. I continued to be thankful for her support, as well as that of my entire family.

A few days after this journey ended, my sister gave birth to a son, Max, who was later joined by a sister, Hallie. This book is dedicated to the two of them, in the hopes that they, too, will go forth on journeys that bring them wisdom from the sands and yield descendants as numerous as the stars.

INDEX